First Facts™

Learning about Money

What Is Money?

by Mary Firestone

Consultant:
Sharon M. Danes, PhD
Professor and Family Economist
University of Minnesota

Capstone
press
Mankato, Minnesota

First Facts is published by Capstone Press
151 Good Counsel Drive, P.O. Box 669, Mankato, Minnesota 56002
www.capstonepress.com

Library of Congress Cataloging-in-Publication Data
Firestone, Mary.
    What is money? / By Mary Firestone.
    p. cm.—(First facts. Learning about money)
    Includes bibliographical references and index.
    ISBN 0-7368-2642-4 (hardcover)
    1. Money—Juvenile literature. I. Title. II. Series.
HG221.5.F57 2005
332.4—dc22   2004000409

Summary: Covers why money is used, currencies of the world, and how bills and coins are made in the United States.

Editorial Credits
Heather Adamson, editor; Jennifer Bergstrom, designer; Enoch Peterson, illustrator; Scott Thoms, photo researcher; Eric Kudalis, product planning editor

Photo Credits
Capstone Press, 8–9 (all); Gary Sundermeyer, 5, 19; Scott Thoms, 20
Comstock Inc., front cover, 1 (all), 13
Corbis/James Leynse, 14
Courtesy of The U.S. Mint, 16, 17 (both)
EyeWire Images, back cover
Getty Images Inc./Stephen Chernin, 11
PhotoDisc Inc., 6
United States Department of the Treasury/Bureau of Engraving and Printing, 15

1 2 3 4 5 6 09 08 07 06 05 04

Table of Contents

Trading

Jim wants Lucy's candy bar. He has an apple to trade. Lucy does not want the apple. She wants an orange.

Without money, people have to **barter**, or trade. Money makes it easier to get what you want. Jim trades Lucy 50 **cents** for the candy bar. She then buys an orange at the lunch counter.

Money Today

People use money to buy things. Buying is like trading. People trade their time and skills for money. Then they trade money for things. Coins and bills are forms of money.

Fun Fact!
Shells, beads, and stones were used as money in many early cultures.

Money around the World

Most countries have their own bills and coins. The money used in a country is called **currency**. The United States, Australia, and Canada call their currencies the dollar. Many European countries use the euro. Mexico uses the peso. Japan uses the yen.

1 Canadian dollar

100 Mexican pesos

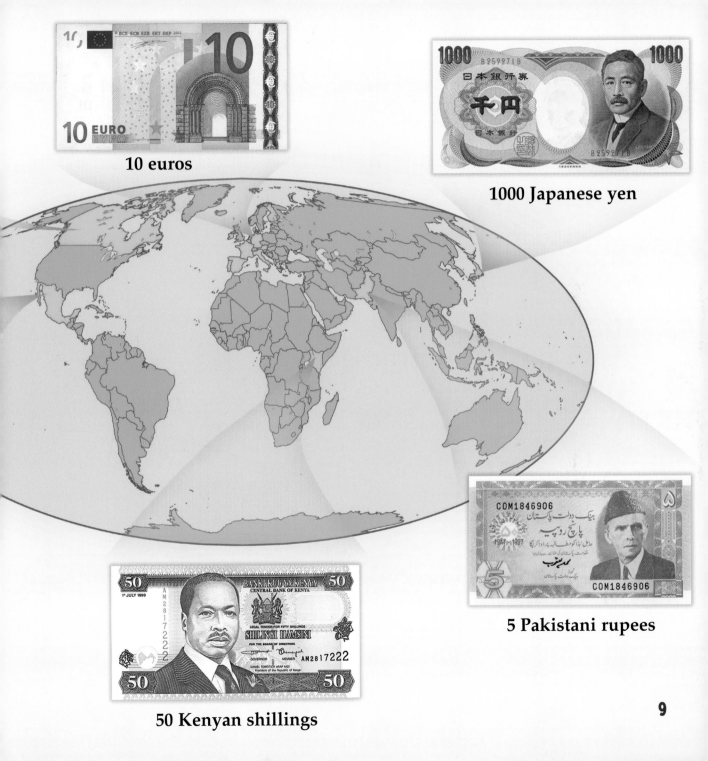

10 euros

1000 Japanese yen

5 Pakistani rupees

50 Kenyan shillings

9

Exchanging Money

Visitors to different countries need the right currency. Visitors to Germany need to trade their money for euros. To trade money, people go to currency **exchanges**. Banks and airports usually have a currency exchange.

Fun Fact!
In early 2004, one U.S. dollar equaled about 11 Mexican pesos.

EXCHANGE RATES

		WE BUY AT	WE SELL AT
AUSTRIA	ATS	14.6	0
BELGIUM	BFR	0	0
CANADA	CAD	1.3	1.2
UNITED KINGDOM	GBP	6	8
FRANCE	FRF	6.9	
GERMANY	DEM	4	0
EURO		1.1	1.2
ITALY	ITL	0	0
JAPAN	JPY	9	90
MEXICO	PESO	0	0
SPAIN	PTS	9	
SWITZERLAND	CHF	3	3

11

Dollars and Cents

Countries divide money into different amounts. They use paper bills and metal coins. A U.S. dollar can be divided into 100 cents. Pennies, nickels, dimes, and quarters are worth different amounts of cents.

Fun Fact!

Coins last much longer than bills. Most coins last 30 years, but most bills last one and a half years.

13

How Bills Are Made

The U.S. Bureau of Engraving and Printing makes paper bills. Inked plates press the bill's design onto large sheets of clothlike paper.

A machine cuts the bills apart.
Thirty-two bills come from each sheet.
The bills are **starched** to make them stiff
and last longer.

How Coins Are Made

U.S. coins are made at **mints**. Metal strips are put into machines called presses. A press punches out coin shapes.

After the blank coins are cleaned, designs are stamped on both sides. The coins fall from the machines into large bins. The coins are inspected before they are used.

Using Money

People use money for things that are important to them. Lucy likes to read. She spends money on books. Lucy's brother likes music. He spends money on CDs. They both think their mom is important. They buy her flowers on her birthday.

Amazing but True!

Many bills have qualities to make them hard to copy. Color-shifting ink on numbers and tiny lines in pictures help people to tell real bills from fake bills. Real bills also show hidden pictures and threads when looked at with lights.

Multicoloring

Hidden Security Thread

Fine-line Printing

Color-shifting Ink

Hands On: Making Change

Store clerks must know the value of each coin and bill. You can learn to count money by practicing making change.

What You Need

markers
small slips of paper
a friend to help
bills and coins
notebook and pencil

What You Do

1. Use markers to write prices on slips of paper. Use different amounts. Spread them out around the room.
2. Give your friend some of the bills and coins. Your friend should go pick up two or three prices.
3. Add up the prices in your notebook. Have your friend pay as if he or she had purchased real items. Write down how much money your friend pays. If the amount paid is more than the amount of the total, you need to make change.
4. Use your bills and coins to pay back change. Now let your friend be the clerk.

Glossary

barter (BAR-tur)—to trade food or goods and services instead of using money

cent (SENT)—a unit of U.S. money; 100 cents equal one dollar.

currency (KUR-uhn-see)—the form of money used in a country

exchange (eks-CHAYNJ)—a place to trade one thing for another; currency exchanges trade one country's money for another.

mint (MINT)—a place where coins are made

starch (STARCH)—to make stiff or hard by using a glue or paste

Read More

Cooper, Jason. *How Coins and Bills Are Made*. Money Power. Vero Beach, Fla.: Rourke, 2003.

Giesecke, Ernestine. *From Seashells to Smart Cards: Money and Currency*. Everyday Economics. Chicago: Heinemann, 2003.

Internet Sites

FactHound offers a safe, fun way to find Internet sites related to this book. All of the sites on FactHound have been researched by our staff.

Here's how:
1. Visit *www.facthound.com*
2. Type in this special code **0736826424** for age-appropriate sites. Or enter a search word related to this book for a more general search.
3. Click on the **Fetch It** button.

FactHound will fetch the best sites for you!

Index